THE SCIENCE OF LIFE

PHOTOSYNTHESIS

by Christine Zuchora-Walske

Content Consultant
Govindjee
Professor Emeritus of Biophysics, Biochemistry, and Plant
Biology, University of Illinois at Urbana-Champaign

CORE
LIBRARY

Published by ABDO Publishing Company, PO Box 398166, Minneapolis, MN 55439. Copyright © 2014 by Abdo Consulting Group, Inc. International copyrights reserved in all countries. No part of this book may be reproduced in any form without written permission from the publisher. The Core Library™ is a trademark and logo of ABDO Publishing Company.

Printed in the United States of America,
North Mankato, Minnesota
102013
012014

♻ THIS BOOK CONTAINS AT LEAST 10% RECYCLED MATERIALS.

Editor: Arnold Ringstad
Series Designer: Becky Daum

Library of Congress Cataloging-in-Publication Data
Zuchora-Walske, Christine.
  Photosynthesis / by Christine Zuchora-Walske.
    pages cm. -- (The science of life)
  Includes bibliographical references and index.
  ISBN 978-1-62403-162-5
1. Photosynthesis--Juvenile literature. I. Title.
  QK882.Z83 2014
  572'.46--dc23

                    2013027630

Photo Credits: Shutterstock Images, cover, 1, 7, 15 (right), 17, 27, 32, 36, 43; NASA, 4; Peter Hermes Furian/Shutterstock Images, 9; Federico Rostagno/Shutterstock Images, 10; Chyrko Olena/Shutterstock Images, 12; Pixel Embargo/Shutterstock Images, 16 (top); Alexander Cherednichenko/Shutterstock Images, 16 (left); Kovalchuk Oleksandr/Shutterstock Images, 16 (middle); Ekaterina V. Borisova/Shutterstock Images, 16 (bottom); Pan Xunbin/Shutterstock Images, 20; BlueRingMedia/Shutterstock Images, 23; Four Oaks/Shutterstock Images, 25; Catalin Petolea/Shutterstock Images, 28; Nikitina Olga/Shutterstock Images, 34; Glenn R. Specht/Shutterstock Images, 38, 45; Fotokostic/Shutterstock Images, 40; Jose Gil/Shutterstock Images, 42 (top); Sebastian Duda/Shutterstock Images, 42 (bottom)

CONTENTS

CHAPTER ONE

EARTH'S ENGINE

As far as we know, Earth is the only planet that is home to living things. That makes Earth a pretty special place.

Lots of processes occur on Earth to make it possible for living things, called organisms, to survive. One of the most important of these processes is photosynthesis. All plants carry out photosynthesis. So do algae and some bacteria. Through this process,

Energy is constantly being moved and used all around the planet.

organisms capture the energy of sunlight. They use this energy to build food from substances in their environment.

Photosynthesis is all about energy. To understand it, it's important to first understand energy.

What Is Energy?

Energy is the engine that drives our universe. It is the ability to do work or to change matter. When energy is used to do work or change matter, that process is known as energy transfer. Every interaction between things transfers energy. Everything in the universe—from the shining of the sun to the blink of your eye—is

Conservation of Energy

The term *conservation of energy* describes how energy behaves. It says that energy is neither created nor destroyed. When energy is released or used during energy transfer, it doesn't disappear. It just changes. For example, when a plant uses the energy of sunlight to make food, that energy does not vanish. It changes into the energy of food.

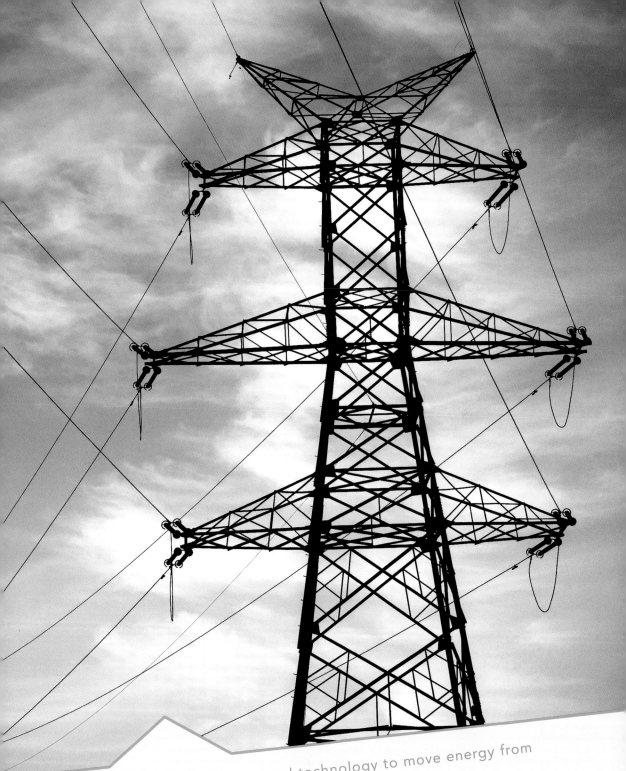

People have developed technology to move energy from place to place.

the result of energy transfer. Energy is constantly on the move. It is never destroyed or created. When it does work or changes matter, it simply turns into a different form.

Solar Energy

On Earth, nearly all of our energy comes from the sun. The sun is a huge ball of gases. Gravity holds the gases together, causing great pressure and heat. The pressure and heat cause the sun to release vast amounts of energy. This energy travels outward in straight lines in every direction. Eventually, some of it reaches Earth. The part of the sun's energy we see and that plants use is called sunlight.

The Solar Spectrum

The sun sends out different kinds of energy. The full range of its energy is called the solar spectrum. Its energy spans nearly the entire electromagnetic spectrum. Part of the solar spectrum includes radio waves similar to those used in radios. Other parts include infrared, visible, and ultraviolet light. Human eyes can only see energy from the visible light part of the solar spectrum.

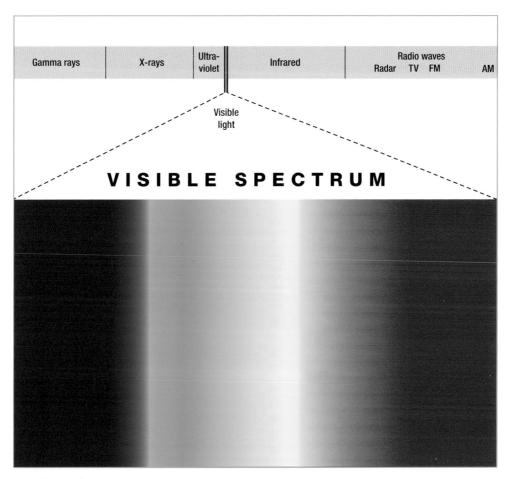

| Gamma rays | X-rays | Ultra-violet | Infrared | Radio waves
Radar TV FM | AM |

Visible
light

VISIBLE SPECTRUM

The Electromagnetic Spectrum
This diagram shows the entire spectrum of electromagnetic radiation. What do you notice about the size of the visible light spectrum compared to the rest of the spectrum?

The sun provides the energy that drives nearly every process on Earth. For example, plants get the energy they need from sunlight. Those plants provide food for other living things and fuel for light

Humans have learned how to get energy from the sun using solar panels, but plants have been doing it for billions of years.

and heat. The sun also warms the land, water, and air in different amounts at different times and places. These temperature differences create ocean currents and weather. The relationship between sunlight and plants is especially important. We'll explore why in Chapter Two.

In his book *Eating the Sun*, journalist Oliver Morton explains how photosynthesis makes life on Earth possible:

> *Here's what happened today. What really happened.*
>
> *Dawn broke. . . .*
>
> *And every time the sunlight hit something green—something truly green, not something painted green or dyed green: something with a greenness that grew—the most important process on the planet began again.*
>
> *When the light shone on the greenness, the greenness welcomed it, and comprehended it, and put it to use. The greenness was chlorophyll, a pigment. It was arranged in pools and the sunlight's energy bounced from one molecule to the next like a frog across lily pads before reaching the subtle trap at the pool's centre, the three-billion-year-old trap where the light of the sun becomes the stuff of the earth. . . .*
>
> *If this process stopped, so would the world.*

Source: Oliver Morton. Eating the Sun. New York: Harper Perennial, 1999.
Print. xi.

What's the Big Idea?

Read this passage from Oliver Morton's book carefully. What is Morton's main point about sunlight, plants, and Earth? Name two or three details that support the main idea.

CHAPTER TWO

PHOTOSYNTHESIS: FOOD FACTORY FOR ALL

The relationship between sunlight and plants is an important one because it makes other processes on Earth possible. Many living things cannot use the sun's energy directly. But plants can. They catch the energy of sunlight to use it themselves and make it available to other organisms.

Plants harness the sun's energy and pass it along to other organisms.

Types of Energy

Energy takes two main forms: kinetic and potential. Things that move, including both objects and light, have kinetic energy. Sunlight is a type of kinetic energy.

Potential energy is energy that has not yet been used. For example, plants capture energy from sunlight. They store some of it as chemical energy. This potential energy exists in the plant's structure. When an animal eats the plant, the energy is released and can do work.

What's in your lunch today? Without peeking, anyone could guess correctly. It's a serving of sunshine. Your friends and family all have the same lunch. So do the neighborhood squirrels, the spiders in your basement, and the dandelions in your yard. In fact, nearly every living thing relies on the sun for food. That's because sunlight is the first link in almost every food chain on Earth. A food chain is a list of living things arranged according to what they eat. Somewhere along the way, your food came from sunlight.

Carrots, Cottontails, and Coyotes

Let's use carrots as an example. The green part of the carrot plant absorbs sunlight. The plant also takes in water from the soil and carbon dioxide from the air. The energy from sunlight powers a chemical reaction in the plant. The water and carbon dioxide molecules break up. They rearrange into sugars and oxygen molecules. The plant

Autotrophs and Heterotrophs

All living things need energy and matter to fuel their growth and survival. Organisms get energy and matter in two basic ways. Autotrophs are living things that can make their own food. Plants, algae, and some bacteria are autotrophs. They get their energy from sunlight and their matter from soil, water, and air. Heterotrophs are organisms that can't make their own food. They must eat other organisms. Animals are heterotrophs. They get both the energy and the matter they need from the organisms they eat.

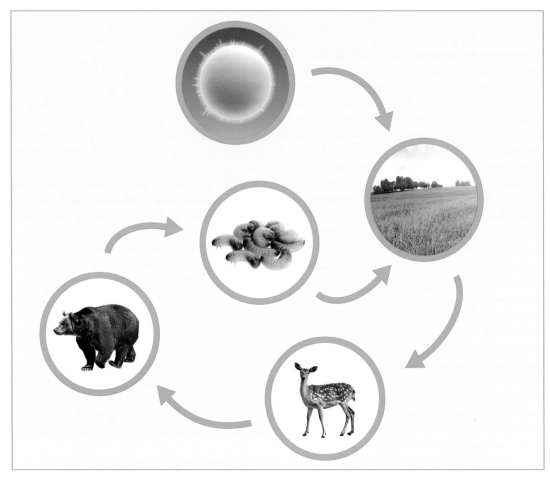

Food Chain

This diagram shows a simple but complete food chain. How does the information presented here compare with what you have learned from the text about food chains? How are they similar? How are they different?

releases the oxygen into the air. It uses the sugar as

food so it can grow and function.

The sugars in the carrot contain chemical energy.

A cottontail rabbit eats the carrot. Chemicals in the

Energy from the sun moves through carrots into rabbits.

EXPLORE ONLINE

The focus of Chapter Two is that plants make the sun's energy available to all other organisms on Earth. It explains that photosynthesizers are the foundation of most food chains. The Web site below also focuses on food chains. As you know, every source is different. How is the information given in the Web site different from the information in this chapter? What information is the same? How do the two sources present information differently? What can you learn from this Web site?

Think Garden: What's a Food Chain?
www.mycorelibrary.com/photosynthesis

rabbit's body break down the carrot and release its chemical energy. The rabbit uses that energy to move and grow.

A coyote then eats the rabbit. Its body breaks down the rabbit and releases energy, which the coyote uses to move and grow. The leftover parts of the rabbit become food for decomposers, such as bacteria. Decomposers are organisms that feed on dead organisms. Decomposers may be microscopic organisms such as bacteria or fungi. They can also be small animals such as ants, beetles, and worms. Decomposers have a dirty job. But it's very important. Decomposers move the chemical energy from organisms back into the soil as nutrients. These nutrients help plants grow.

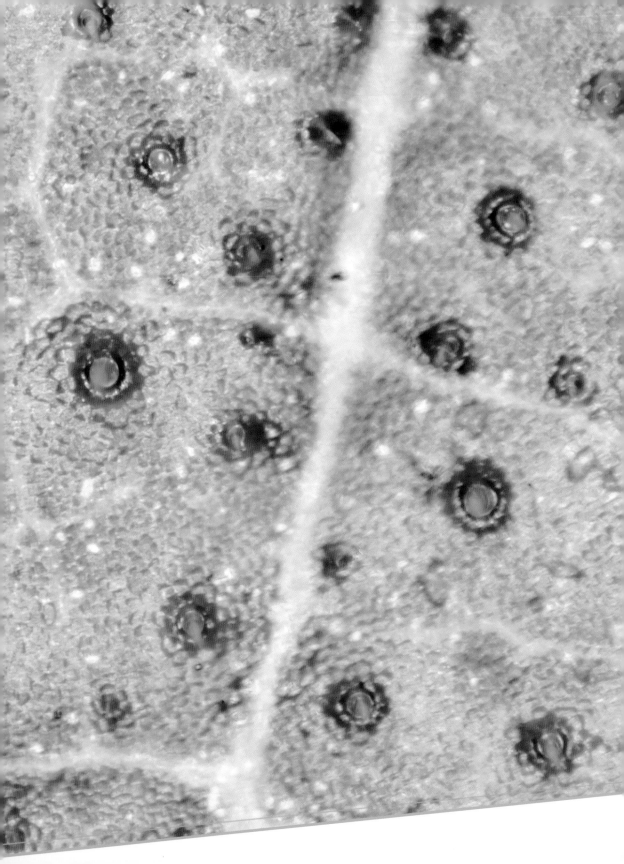

CHAPTER THREE

INSIDE THE FOOD FACTORY

So how exactly do plants and other organisms that use photosynthesis make their own food? In order to understand photosynthesis, it's important to first understand the key parts inside these organisms that make it possible. Let's use plants as an example since we see plants around us every day.

Plant cells are visible under a microscope.

Structure of a Chloroplast

Like all organisms, plants are made up of cells. Photosynthesis occurs mostly inside a layer of cells in the leaves. The cells are rich in chloroplasts. These green-colored structures are where photosynthesis happens.

Each chloroplast contains many sacs called thylakoids. The thylakoids are flat, circular disks. They are arranged in stacks. Each stack is called a granum. Groups of stacks are called grana. The space between grana is filled with a gooey substance called stroma.

Inside each thylakoid are pigments. These are

Chlorophylls and Carotenoids

Plants contain two main types of pigments: chlorophylls and carotenoids. Chlorophylls reflect green light, so they appear green. Carotenoids reflect orange and yellow light, so they appear orange and yellow. During spring and summer, chlorophylls give leaves a green color. Leaves stop making chlorophylls when the weather becomes cool. When that happens, the leaves no longer reflect green light. Instead, they reflect orange and yellow light.

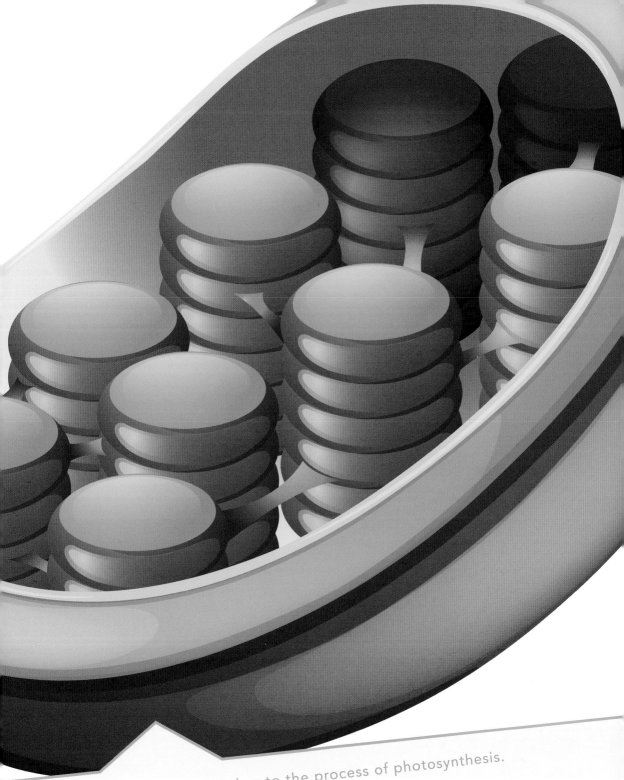

Chloroplasts are key to the process of photosynthesis.

molecules that are good at absorbing visible light. The light they reflect gives them their color. The pigment molecules are bunched together in groups and held in place by protein molecules. Proteins are the materials that make up organisms' structures. Each group of proteins and pigments inside a thylakoid is called a photosystem.

How a Photosystem Captures Sunlight

The first steps in photosynthesis are the light-dependent reactions. These begin with light from the sun. Within a

Billiards Break

Think of the energy transfer from pigment molecule to pigment molecule like the beginning break in a game of billiards. Fifteen colored balls are arranged, touching one another, in a snug triangle on the pool table. A player shoots the white cue ball, representing the energy of sunlight. It hits the point of the triangle and the two balls at the far corners of the triangle fly off, but none of the central balls move. The energy simply passes through the central balls to the most distant ones.

Energy movement through photosystems can be compared to the movement of energy around a pool table.

photosystem, each pigment molecule can capture visible light, which arrives in tiny particles called photons. When a photon strikes a pigment molecule, the molecule absorbs it. The photon's energy then passes from that pigment molecule to another one that's nearby. The energy continues moving from one pigment molecule to the next.

Eventually the passed-along energy arrives at a group of proteins and pigments called the reaction center. The reaction center transfers the energy into two chemicals called ATP and NADPH. These chemicals are used by cells for energy storage. Two different photosystems are used to create ATP and NADPH.

Building Organic Molecules

When the proteins receive stored energy in ATP and NADPH from the photosystem, they put that energy to work. The proteins use ATP and NADPH to build organic molecules. This happens

ATP and NADPH

ATP and NADPH are complicated molecules. ATP stands for adenosine triphosphate. One molecule is made up of ten carbon atoms, sixteen hydrogen atoms, five nitrogen atoms, thirteen oxygen atoms, and three phosphorus atoms. NADPH stands for nicotinamide adenine dinucleotide phosphate. Each molecule contains twenty-one carbon atoms, twenty-nine hydrogen atoms, seven nitrogen atoms, seventeen oxygen atoms, and three phosphorus atoms.

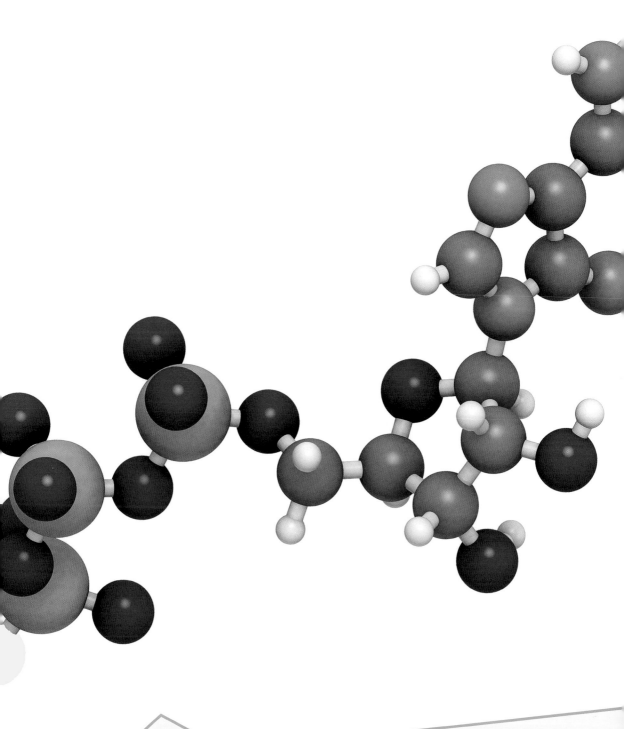

ATP molecules transfer energy throughout the human body.

Some types of plants, such as apple trees, store energy inside fruit.

during the light-independent reactions. Unlike the earlier part of photosynthesis, they do not require light to carry out.

Organic molecules are molecules that contain carbon atoms. They join together easily, which makes them useful for building complex structures. They provide energy and matter for the plant's body, helping it grow and function.

Plant proteins build organic molecules through a process called the Calvin-Benson cycle. This process is named after its discoverers, Melvin Calvin and Andrew Benson. The cycle takes place outside the thylakoid, in the gooey stroma that

The Human Battery

Human beings also use ATP to move energy from place to place within their bodies. On average, the human body contains just about 0.55 pounds (250 g) of ATP at any given time. This provides about the same amount of energy as a typical AA battery. However, the ATP is constantly being used and recycled to provide energy to different parts of the body.

fills the chloroplast. Water, carbon dioxide, ATP, and NADPH work together to create a simple sugar. The plant's cells then use this sugar to build a wide variety of other sugars and organic molecules, including glucose. These products travel throughout the plant. The plant uses them for growth, for fuel, and for carrying out its everyday functions.

German scientist Julius Mayer made the following observations in an 1845 pamphlet titled *The Organic Motion in Its Relation to Metabolism*:

> *Nature has put itself the problem how to catch in flight light streaming to the earth and to store the most elusive of all powers in rigid form. To achieve this aim, it has covered the crust of earth with organisms which in their life processes absorb the light of the sun and use this power to produce a continuously accumulating chemical difference.*
>
> *These organisms are the plants; the plant kingdom forms a reservoir in which the fleeting sun rays are fixed and skillfully stored for future use; an economic provision to which the physical existence of mankind is inexorably bound.*
>
> *Source: Eugene Rabinowitch and Govindjee. Photosynthesis. New York: Wiley, 1969. Web. Accessed August 20, 2013.*

Consider Your Audience

Review this passage closely. It was published when scientists used different terms than modern scientists use. For example, Mayer used the term *power* where we would say *energy*, and *chemical difference* where we would say *chemical energy*. Write a blog post giving this information so a modern audience can understand it. How does your new approach differ from the original text, and why?

CHAPTER FOUR

THE KEY TO LIFE

Photosynthesis is the key to life on Earth. It's the process that holds us all together as a global ecosystem. An ecosystem is a group of living and nonliving things that interact with one another in a specific environment. An ecosystem can be as small as a tide pool or as big as a planet. The organisms in an ecosystem depend on one another and affect one another.

Photosynthesis helps move gases and water through ecosystems.

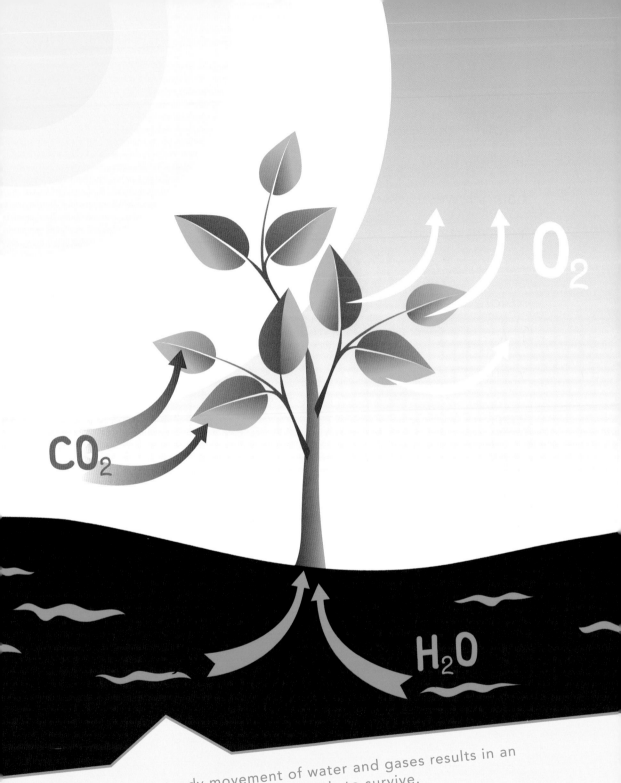

O₂

CO₂

H₂O

The steady movement of water and gases results in an ideal environment for animals to survive.

Photosynthesis is the process that drives all the other processes of life. This is partly because photosynthesis is the first link in nearly every food chain. However, that is not the whole picture. Life on Earth depends on the constant cycling of energy and matter through our ecosystem. We've already explored the role of photosynthesis in cycling energy. Now let's look at the role photosynthesis plays in cycling matter.

Cycling Water

Organisms need water, oxygen, and carbon dioxide to function. These types of matter must keep moving around on Earth to provide a constant supply for living things to use. Photosynthesis helps keep them moving.

In the water cycle, sunlight causes water to evaporate from bodies of water and from living things. The evaporated water becomes water vapor in the atmosphere, forming clouds. When the vapor cools, it forms water droplets, which fall as rain or

Without the greenhouse effect holding heat in the atmosphere, Earth might be too cold to support life.

snow. Some of this water evaporates right away, some soaks into the ground and becomes groundwater, and some runs off into bodies of water. Plants drink up water from the soil through their roots, and that water travels through veins to the leaves. There, it plays a crucial role in photosynthesis.

Cycling Gases

The gases in the atmosphere are responsible for making the Earth able to support life. Plants play a big role in keeping the gases in

Our Global Greenhouse

Sunlight passes easily through our atmosphere to Earth. Snow, ice, and clouds reflect some of this energy back into space. But land, water, trees, buildings, and other objects absorb a lot of it. As they do, Earth's surface warms up. The warm surface radiates heat. Some of it escapes into space. But certain gases in the atmosphere—especially water vapor and carbon dioxide—absorb heat. These gases radiate some of the heat back to the ground. The overall effect traps heat in the atmosphere. This heat-trapping process is called the greenhouse effect. It keeps Earth warm enough to make life possible.

In the water cycle, water moves from the clouds to the ground and back again.

balance. Water is made up of hydrogen and oxygen. The plant uses the energy from the sunlight to separate the oxygen and hydrogen in water. The oxygen exits the leaves through tiny openings called stomata. Leftover water absorbed by the plant is simply released back into the atmosphere as water vapor.

A plant stores some of the sugars it has made and uses the rest for energy. When that plant is eaten, the cells of the animal eating it

A Delicate Balance

Plants give other organisms food and oxygen, two key tools for survival. Meanwhile, other organisms give plants carbon dioxide through the air and nutrients in the soil. Trouble can result when oxygen and carbon dioxide go out of balance. Human activities, such as driving cars and operating power plants, put extra carbon dioxide into the atmosphere. At the same time, people are cutting down many forests. As a result, plants can't keep up with the extra carbon dioxide. The amount of carbon dioxide in the atmosphere is going up. Since more carbon dioxide radiates more of the sun's heat back to Earth, the planet is gradually warming.

Plants give us the energy and oxygen we need to do all kinds of activities.

use oxygen to break down the plant's tissues during digestion. This releases stored carbon into the animal's body. As the animal breathes out, it releases carbon dioxide into the air. Plants take in the carbon dioxide through their stomata, and the cycle begins again.

Plant Power

During photosynthesis, electrons are freed from water molecules using light energy. These electrons then go toward producing sugars for the plant's survival. In other words, the light energy turns into chemical energy. Scientists are investigating ways to use the processes that happen in photosynthesis—both natural and artificial—to generate power for human use instead. Several research groups are working on ways to channel the flow of these electrons into wires as electricity. Other groups are modifying photosynthesis so it creates hydrogen. They are then using this hydrogen to create fuel.

Some cars are powered by hydrogen fuel cells.

Photosynthetic Medicine

Photosynthesis uses the energy from sunlight to transform carbon dioxide and water into sugar and oxygen. That process also produces many chemical compounds. Scientists are exploring ways to change the way this process works. They predict it may be possible to make different chemicals using chloroplasts. These other chemicals have potential uses in medicines and other products.

Scientific research on photosynthesis has the potential to change our everyday lives.

Hydroponics gives farmers extra control over plant growing conditions.

Hydroponics

Hydroponics is a type of farming in which people grow plants without soil. Hydroponic farmers simply dissolve into water the nutrients that plants normally get from the soil. Already, many gardeners in areas with scarce or expensive land are using hydroponics to grow crops underground, on rooftops, and in greenhouses. Plants can also be grown outside their regular growing seasons. As the human population soars and farmable land dwindles, hydroponics may become more important.

STOP AND THINK

Why Do I Care?

Your body doesn't carry out photosynthesis. But that doesn't mean you don't depend on this process. How does photosynthesis in plants affect your life as an animal? Could you exist without photosynthesis? What would happen to the environment and the organisms on Earth if plants somehow lost the ability to carry out photosynthesis? Use your imagination!

Take a Stand

This book discusses the importance of balance in our global ecosystem. Most scientists believe that human activities are upsetting the delicate give-and-take that takes place among organisms and the environment. Do you agree? Can you think of some ways in which humans might be harming Earth? Write a short essay explaining your opinion. Make sure to give reasons for your opinion, and facts and details that support those reasons.

Tell the Tale

Imagine that you are a farmer in the city who is growing vegetables hydroponically. Write 200 words describing the benefits of your work.

Dig Deeper

After reading this book, what questions do you still have about photosynthesis? Write down one or two questions that can guide you in doing research. With an adult's help, find a few reliable sources that can help answer your questions. Write a few sentences about your research.

GLOSSARY

ATP and NADPH
short for adenosine triphosphate and nicotinamide adenine dinucleotide phosphate, two chemicals used by cells for energy storage

chloroplasts
parts of cells in which photosynthesis occurs

glucose
a sugar produced during photosynthesis

organic molecules
molecules that contain carbon atoms and are useful for forming complex structures

photosystems
clusters of pigment molecules and proteins within a thylakoid that work together to trap sunlight and store its energy

pigments
molecules that are good at absorbing visible light

stomata
tiny openings on the undersides of the leaves that take in carbon dioxide and emit oxygen

stroma
a gooey semiliquid substance that fills the space between grana

thylakoids
flat, circular disks inside a chloroplast, often arranged in stacks called grana

LEARN MORE

Books

Bang, Molly, and Penny Chisholm. *Living Sunlight: How Plants Bring the Earth to Life*. New York: Blue Sky Press, 2009.

Encyclopedia of Nature. New York: DK, 2007.

Web Links

To learn more about photosynthesis, visit ABDO Publishing Company online at **www.abdopublishing.com**. Web sites about photosynthesis are featured on our Book Links page. These links are routinely monitored and updated to provide the most current information available. Visit **www.mycorelibrary.com** for free additional tools for teachers and students.

INDEX

ABOUT THE AUTHOR

Christine Zuchora-Walske has been writing and editing books for children, parents, and teachers for more than 20 years. She lives in Minneapolis, Minnesota, with her husband and two children.